RARA AVIS

Also by Blas Falconer

Poems

Forgive the Body This Failure
The Foundling Wheel
A Question of Gravity and Light

Edited Anthologies

Mentor and Muse: Essays from Poets to Poets (with Beth Martinelli and Helena Mesa)
The Other Latin@: Writing Against a Singular Identity (with Lorraine M. López)

RARA AVIS

Blas Falconer

Four Way Books
Tribeca

For you. For the you before you and the one before that.

Library of Congress Cataloging-in-Publication Data

Names: Falconer, Blas, author.
Title: Rara Avis / Blas Falconer.
Other titles: Rara Avis (Compilation)
Description: New York : Four Way Books, 2024.
Identifiers: LCCN 2024000659 (print) | LCCN 2024000660 (ebook) | ISBN
9781961897021 (trade paperback) | ISBN 9781961897038 (epub)
Subjects: LCGFT: Poetry.
Classification: LCC PS3606.A425 R37 2024 (print) | LCC PS3606.A425
(ebook) | DDC 811/.6--dc23/eng/20240111
LC record available at https://lccn.loc.gov/2024000659
LC ebook record available at https://lccn.loc.gov/2024000660

This book is manufactured in the United States of America and printed on
acid-free paper.

Four Way Books is a not-for-profit literary press. We are grateful for the assistance
we receive from individual donors, public arts agencies, and private foundations
including the New York State Council on the Arts, a state agency.

We are a proud member of the Community of Literary Magazines and Presses.

Contents

Rara Avis

A falcon, one of millions raised
for sacrifice. An X-ray

reveals the bird, _un-tombed_,
wrapped in linen, wings pressed

the length of its ghostly body.
Force-fed mice, sparrows, it couldn't

expel the bones, the claws,
and died having eaten too much,

the stomach packed: feather and
fur, tail descending the throat.

One of many bred to brave
the dark with its king, beyond

appetite, nothing left
to crave, thus, heavenly, saved.

love the hybrid meshing of prefixes

Beautiful enjambment

alliteration

1

Pancreas

A gland, like

          a sponge,
      secreting fluids to

regulate

          blood sugar, to
      break down.

Common

          ailments include
      inflammation (*pan-*

creatitis) and

          cancer (ab-
      dominal pain,

weight loss,

          jaundice). It's
      possible to live

without one, my

          father says
      on the phone, a

dryness in

        his mouth, his

    tongue sticking as

he tells me what

        to expect if

    he's lucky. And

all day, everything,

        no matter how

    small, makes me

think of it,

        hidden deep

    inside me,

weeping. The bee

        crawling in

    blossoms

scattered on

        the glass

    tabletop. The sound of

[handwritten annotation:]) beautiful transion— anatomy to natural world

a pitcher fill-

                ing slowly

    with water.

A faded picture of our father and

you with whom I no longer speak,
taken before I was born, before

we fell out, before he grew sick.
Weeks ago, my neighbor and his wife

fought in their front yard. *You don't
love me anymore. You haven't loved me*

in years. What could he say? The photo,
fifty years old—how did it come to be

mine, our father in his green shirt,
and faintly, the face you will

grow into. What am I to do with it?

Providence

We leaned back
            in the planetarium
      seats, looking up

into the dark—
            a father and his
      two sons. We heard

what could have been
            God, the universe,
      an actor reading from

a script. He told us where
            we came from, where
      we were among

infinite specks of light.
            The boys grew
      animated, silhouettes

pointing to
            constellations, heads
      leaning closer, more

questions
        wanting answers.
    The younger crawled

into my lap,
        the older held
    my hand

under the great
        black dome.
    When the lights

came on, my sons stared
        at the large blank screen.
    Everyone

stood up. I began
        searching for
    my keys.

third to
1st person

Qué Significa

I thought it'd be cooler, here, in late June,
but all night I'm kicking off the sheets
and pulling them back over my body in the stillness
of my room until I remember, suddenly,
those summers as a boy, lying in the twin bed
with you. That was before the highway, when
one needed to drive up and down the mountains
to get from one side of the island to the other, and
Salinas, where the fishing nets hung to dry
in branches along the shore and we swam
in a clearing among the mangroves or rocked
in a hammock behind the house where my mother and
your father were born, still seemed untouched
by "America." Sometimes, at the bakery, or with
the woman who sold lottery tickets outside
the restaurant, or as the men drove us in the back
of their trucks past the sugarcane fields, not understanding
a word or turn of phrase, a joke someone made,
I'd ask, *Qué significa*, but it was already
over or too hard to explain, you'd say. I grew
homesick for English. One summer, at the movies,
you cried so hard it scared me, the screen lighting your wet face.
One summer, sprawled out on the floor in front
of the TV in our bathing suits, we began

to wrestle, laughing until our hands, then our mouths
moved across our bodies, driven by a force we let
guide us. Then someone stopped, and we lay
in the sunlit room breathing hard. Someone must have
gotten up and walked away. Someone must have made
small talk until we could pretend it never happened.
Quiero verte, you said on the phone
years later both of us now with children
of our own. And when I made it back one day
to the island, I drove to your house, knocking on
the large door at the agreed-upon time,
but no one answered. The flamboyant trees
were in bloom, their bright red blossoms scattered on
the street, and it didn't take long to get back
to my hotel, but I got lost. I'd never been
to that part of the city and so much had changed.

Nights I lay in bed, the drunks below

calling in the dark, the loud music of a radio
fading in the distance as
I fell asleep. I never saw the hurricanes

of late summer hit shore, only the swell
before, the still surface after, storefronts

boarded with plywood and
corrugated metal, trash heaped and lit
on fire, black horns of smoke

dissipating in the early morning. How
young, how ignorant,

sucking clusters of Spanish limes
in the shade, spitting out seeds, ready to trust
anyone who stopped on the road sparkling with

broken bottles tossed from car windows.
They made room, and I slid

into the cabin's seat, the whole truck
trembling with the engine's power, the end of the gear
humming in the driver's palm. My leg pressed

against his, so when he punched
the clutch and hit the gas, his thigh's

coarse hair brushed mine and I
lunged forward, sugarcane fields
stretching out, sweet and green, on either side.

A Theory on Happiness

Driving along the coast
in a convertible, the sea

behind them, one will make
a vow—for better

or worse. *Will I be
happy*, he asks,

guiding the car
along the cliff's edge,

and the friend, who is
somewhat older, says, *Yes,*

*you will be happy but
you will not know it.*

Kindness

He's kind because he wants people to
like him, Mary's mother said. The first
woman in Italy to earn a PhD
in Chemistry, and whose family survived
the war by hiding hens on the patio
of their apartment, she knew I'd just
come out of the closet at 24,
and, loathing myself, saw any kindness
an act of great charity for which I
should be grateful, so maybe she was right,
but her insight became another reason
to hate myself. Mary and I taught
in Tatabánya, Hungary that year, where
we earned 200 dollars a month, but
she'd lost her job and come to live with me
in a studio on the edge of town.
I met Mike and traveled as far as Miskolc,
the other end of the country, to let
him touch me, which was the first time I'd been
touched by a man without feeling fear.
Mary lost so much weight that her thick hair
started falling out. She'd run her fingers
across her scalp, and let the clumps float
to the floor. *See?* When we left, her hair

explains
earlier
poem

grew back. She went to law school but wanted
to get married, have a family more
than anything else. In our mid 30s, I went
to her house where she lived with her husband,
a military pilot, and two kids.
She was a judge, and our friend Ivy, who
we'd known as long as we'd known
each other, had come, too. *I believe that,*
constitutionally, you have the right
to marry a man, Mary told me, *but*
I vote for whomever lets me keep
as much of my money as possible.
She went on to say, slicing a piece of cheese
for her cracker, how difficult it'd be
to get along without her au pair, whose
two-year visa was ending, and soon would have
to go back to France if she didn't find
an American husband—and would I
consider it? Ivy looked embarrassed
as I stumbled in confusion—that I later
recognized as anger—to remind Mary
that I was living with Joseph, the man
I loved. We didn't talk again until
2011, when she told me

Ivy had died, and was surprised to hear
that I suspected it was why she was calling
after so much time. A few months before,
Ivy left a message to congratulate us
about the adoption—*I'm so happy, so*
so happy for you both—and that she had
cancer and hoped to beat it, but when
she didn't answer my calls, I feared
the worst. As far as Mary knew, Ivy hadn't told
anyone else. *She must have really liked you,*
Mary said to herself, it seemed, as much
as to me, and I felt I should say
something kind in return, but took
a deep breath wondering how to begin.

Son

—For my son, who asks to live with us forever

When the car stopped in front of the house that night
        after the long drive, my father lifted me

from the back seat. *He's awake*, my brother said,
        Asleep, my sister, their small shoes turning stones

on the narrow path. I didn't open my eyes
        but could smell my father's breath, warm and sweet.

Is not, Is too—they argued as I floated like
        a dream through the dark above them,

cradled under the great branch. The roots pushed deeper
        into the soft ground. I was neither, of course,

or both. The sound of the key as it entered the lock.
        The sound of the door swinging open. Closed.

*

We haven't left the house in months, touching
        almost no one else, and you fall asleep

holding my hand until your breathing grows

      long and steady, your face soft as if

you've gone some place I can't. My own

      father lies in a hospital on the other side

of the country, and through the phone,

      over the sound of machines, nurses, their

questions, his voice grows weaker, telling me

      what he won't. Like the day you dove

to the bottom of the pool, that stillness

      on the surface, me holding my breath.

Or the summer my father, in a small boat

      with the white sail and simple red star,

skimmed back and forth along the shore, where I stood,

      waiting. Years from now, I'll be telling you

this: *Forgive me, Son.* How can I spare you from

      what I have not been spared?

Long Gone

Because the boys
           will not stop
      fighting, I hit

the brakes and
           turn around,
      staring them

down, the words,
           loud and cruel,
      rushing from

my mouth, until they
           cower in
      their seats, and when

I'm done, angrier
           than even I
      understand,

the younger says,
           He scared me,
      as if I'm not

there, the way years

    from now, driving,

  he might confess—*He*

scared me

    sometimes—to his

  brother, the road

ending abruptly

    at a field of trees

  they can't see through

and must guess

    instead what lies

  beyond it.

Reconciliation, back then, meant

forgiving the offense,

                whatever it was,

whatever it was I was

                forgiven for.

For a Spell

—For T. C. (1970-2008)

You dip the end of the small plastic wand
into the soapy water, hold it

to your mouth, and blow gently, so
the iridescent film

within the serrated ring
trembles as it grows and grows, until

you are——*we are*——in it,
all that *has ever* or *will ever* waits

outside the bubble, which floats, now,
slowly to the ground.

                              *

When a bubble floats to the ground
it means something is about

to break. A spell can be
broken. We say, *You fall*

under a spell the way
we say, *You fall*

in love. For a spell means an undefined
but short period of time,

as in, *For a spell, we didn't want*
anything else.

On Parting

—After Masaccio's *Expulsion from the Garden*

How light fell on a wall where
a man and woman, forsaken in

a desert, were painted to look
as if lit by the chapel's one

window, so the shadows
of those driven out of the garden

fell beside the shadow of anyone
who'd come to stand before them—

you recall one night, after many years,
walking beneath a neighbor's tree,

the great cluster of fruit
shining beneath the streetlamp,

bearing the branch so low
your impulse was to take it.

*

The branch snapping back from
the hand. Small leaves trembling. The urge

to hold the fruit to your face and breathe,
drunk with the outer edge of its

ripeness, like a secret you need
to share with someone who needs

to share it, too. They walk out
of the garden, his heel on the threshold,

and keep walking, generation
after generation, until *before*

seems more like a dream you had,
only a story someone told you once,

but here you are, again, walking away
from what you thought you always wanted.

Forgiven

—After Rembrandt's *The Return of the Prodigal Son*

When the shoulders of the man sitting in front of me
are the width of your shoulders, the slouch

your slouch, I think,
this time, to lean into the sting

of your leaving, the way
you, long dead now, once leaned over a sink,

the smell of shaving cream, your own face
in the mirror, a speck

of blood spreading in white foam.
We sat there for nearly an hour, me and not-you

and the poet onstage who said:
a snow globe shaken relives the same

shatter. Years later, I can not want you
and not want you to have left.

＊

I held your waist
and we rocked slowly under our studio's

one window, which glowed
　　　with the morning paper

　　you taped there so
neighbors couldn't see. News *Interesting placement*

of storms hitting the coast,
that summer, news of war. One night,

you stormed off at dinner,
　　　　　　shaking your head,

　　　your fists. You had your own
ghosts—you, who'd held

a spoon of ice cream, cold and sweet,
to my mouth, singing—*open up*—softly.

reoccurring Theme

Forgiveness was the moral of the story,
and the master's depiction,

which has been said to bring those
who come upon it to tears: one man

kneeling, his shorn head pressed
into the other's robes. In the painting

the young man's clothes are tattered,
his shoe has fallen off, his bare foot

exposed. The light spills on both men
       from an open door,

somewhere beyond our view,
            which the one

      who has only now,
after so many years, come through.

On what has become of his body

—A cento after *The Long Answer* by David Keplinger

The saddest trains go north
through darkness
like a cup or a pocketknife
I have wanted to save
that was my first weapon
It's now so late
it's almost morning
Ladies and Gentlemen
He has time
we are somewhere in a story
There is a point of singularity
the train is coming east. In the window
is a luminous egg
Why do you think I'm so happy

*

Why do you think I'm so happy
I want to think I'm someone else
and take small sips until he shows me
me, the eyes all scissored out
the heart into the smallest particles
backwards, out of view
When I met him at the door

His eyes met my eyes and pushed part way through
the work still loud in his body
You may find that you are lost
the bus shoves off
although I can't say where
Your tiny mouth parted. The hook slipped down your throat
like the answer

*

like the answer
I went back to doing what I'd been doing all day
by dark we had made a little clearing
Winter is early. We are surprised
at nothing
I have known
our stories in great loops, each practiced letter
sureness, their ardor to die
when they came to a stop
because I was the only one left in the room
the rest is tenderness
She calls her horses back through the dark
Where is he now, my Jacob
You must have had some place to go so I let you go

Before surgery, I remember

how the bone

        broke, the forearm hung

    where it shouldn't have,

and the boy

        looked at it with

    confusion, then

horror. Someone ran

        for ice, someone

    lowered him

to the ground, and we stood

        watching, trying not

    to watch him turn

pale and

        tremble with shock.

    A man knelt

beside him and spoke

        into his ear, so

    no one else

could hear, and the boy

nodded, closing

his eyes. A calm

fell over his face,

until the place he lay

became the place

he no longer lay. Now,

all day, someone

is crying and

trying not to.

Someone is crying

and trying not to.

Is there anything else

I need to tell you,

the doctor asks,

before you go

under. The knife

pierces the skin. Two sides

part, open and open and—.

Tell me. What more

can you tell me?

My Son Wants to Know Who His Biological Father Is

My son wants to know
his name. *What does he look like? What does*
he like? My son swims
four days a week. When my son swims
underwater, he glides
between strokes. When he glides underwater, he is
an arrow aimed
at a wall. Four days a week, his coach says,
Count—1...2...—before
coming up for air.
My father had blue eyes, blond hair,
though mine are brown.
My father could not speak
Spanish and wondered, *How can you love*
another man? We rarely touched.
When my son
is counting, I count
with him. I say, *I am*
your father, too. 1...2...

Heredity

In the book we read, Gregor Mendel notes
selected traits

        (flower color, stalk height)
of plants, and hand-drawn

            illustrations show
the friar bend to his subjects, so

           a child

can learn how selected traits—

         color, height—
of offspring are determined by

          the parents,
    and how to study a subject: the child,
himself, part of

      a mathematical pattern.

Determined by his biological parents,
who they are, or what, at least,

        they look like,
my son is part

     of a mathematical pattern
for which he only has

the answers: eyes,

hair. . . We can guess
         what they look like—
see *Segregation*,
         Mendel's first genetic law—
working backwards for
         the answer—his eyes:
brown, his hair: brown—
         thanks to the father

of genetics, and
         Dominance, his third law
of inheritance. Illustrations show
my son how to draw the image of
         that father,
to read the book
         his body writes,
         the notes.

Fatherland

The heat not having broken all
month long, we stood

in line and watched a boy
race down the park's tallest slide,

drop into the shallow pool
below, from which he rose

renewed, a look of joy, relief
across his face. My son held

my hand, and looking up,
judged how long it'd take

to reach the top of the stairs.
In front of us, the man, a head

taller, fifty pounds, at least,
more than I, wore red trunks,

his hair dark brown, short.
I saw the swastika first,

White Power inked
across his back, the scene:

skeletons climbed his spine
above a sea of flames. I felt

each breakable bone
in my boy's hand, he who

days before asked to live
with us forever. *Idiot,*

my mother called me once,
because *you think everyone*

is good. The man looked
across the park at no one,

younger than I'd have thought,
and when the line, as if

with one mind, began to move
again, he stepped forward, the foot

or two between us
perilous, uncrossable.

Figura Serpentinata

She began screaming at
the man standing behind us

in line. The cashier looked
out from behind a glass

partition. The man stepped
back laughing, shaking

his head. *Stop,* I said
to my mother. *Please.* I was

still a child. She was still
screaming, *He can't touch me*

like that. The men looked
to each other and looked

away. Then she stopped,
electrified with rage, took

my hand, and we stood
in silence, waiting to pay.

＊

My father and I sat
at the kitchen table when

we heard, faintly, someone
screaming. *Your sister*, he said

alarmed, already leaping up
the stairs, and for a moment,

I too imagined someone
standing over her in the dark.

Dad, I called, and he stopped
on the landing outside

her door. *It's just a song
on the radio*—so low that we

couldn't discern the words.
A song, I repeated. *That's all.*

We walked back down the steps
breathless, shaking our heads.

*

In Giambologna's *Abduction*,
the figures move upward

in a twisting pattern known
as *figura serpentinata*.

One man straddles another as
he carries the woman away.

Where he grabs her left hip,
fingers press into her flesh.

The woman, arms outstretched,
turns back as she is hoisted in

the air. You must engage
the sculpture in 360 degrees

to see the drama unfold. When the work
was unveiled to the public

in August of 1582, not one
person could find fault with it.

Impressionism

The framed painting in the hallway outside
my office is the size of a postcard
or small windowpane, so you must stop
and bend close to see the brushstrokes
in brown and white are five horses coming
to the edge of a lake, maybe a river. If
their bodies in oil on a canvas panel are
the suggestion of the Paso Finos, then
their reflections in the water are little more
than a smudge, a finger grazing the scene
of early morning, the sky overcast above the rocks,
tall grass, a palm, and in the background, what might
be sugarcane, which once spread across the fields
before the harvest. *W. Torres,*
the artist, in the lower right-hand corner. *Wichie,*
she said when I asked as a boy the day
I first found the picture in a dresser drawer
in my grandmother's apartment over the shops,
one block from the square, and where, in the back bedroom,
older cousins held me down—*Say it, say you're
a girl*—punching me if I did, punching me
if I didn't. Each year, I'd find it
somewhere else, unframed, on a high shelf,
among scattered magazines and pocket change,

by the phone, where she'd written on the back
some scribble to see if a pen had ink
before writing something down quick,
a number to call or address of some place
she needed to go. We didn't talk much,
my Spanish no good, her English worse,
at the restaurant where she worked. *Get out*
of my way, she complained if I tried to help,
and I waited by the car for her to lock
the doors each night. I cried at the end
of each summer, saying goodbye, and she'd laugh,
look at me wide-eyed, unblinking as if I were some
strange animal. In my twenties, I'd spend the whole day
at a table overlooking the ocean and watch
fishermen motor out, then in. Between the afternoon
and evening rush, she'd bring a plate of food
that she'd made: pescado al mojo, arroz
con gandules, mofongo relleno. *Put the book*
down, she'd say. *Eat.* She would stand there,
waiting to see if I liked it. She would stand there,
an odd look on her face, as if she were trying to
remember what she wanted to tell me. Then,
without a word, she'd turn and walk away.

Where It Hurts

—For Carmen Correa

Where do you go when you
forget who you are? You sit

at the window, and neighbors stop—
Pilar, the seamstress to say,

Hello—Hector, *Goodbye.* Each time
a shop door opens, small bells

chime. In the morning, name-
less mountains rise, and at night,

I carry you to bed. Before you die,
you wake in fits of pain,

delusions. Mother asks where
it hurts. *Here,* you cry, *and here.*

Legacy

Nearly all
           my mother deemed
      worth keeping until now

makes its way
          across a sea,
     a continent:

the piano, the brass bed,
          the painting of
   horses

hung in
         the hallway of
     her mother's house.

A great tree grew
         in the center of
    the yard, she said

once. *Almendras.*
        Imagine it,
    the glass bowl, too—

so small, what could

        it hold?—wrapped in

    tissue to travel a

century, a

        language, boxed

    with whatever else

she can't take,

        coming to break me

    faster.

Like a Prize, Like a Black Pearl

I woke up in the middle of the night to the sound
    of my friend in the next room crying.

For whom or what, I wondered, looking out
    the window. *I wish that I could be there*, I said

into the receiver the last time I spoke to my father.
    If only it were as simple as reaching

into the body, plucking out like a prize, like a black pearl,
    pain. I imagined my friend in the dark,

the sheet between his fists, gasping for air between sobs.
    There was a time when I thought I could bear

anything. Now, the phone rings, and——. They'll make
    the midline incision from the breastbone,

the length of his stomach. Some nights, when everyone
    is sleeping, I stand in the yard and let the dog

root through the bushes for whatever has made
    a home for itself there. The branches shake

[handwritten annotations: "surprising", "like", "break", "beautiful alliteration", "reoccurring theme of surgery"]

as she pushes herself through the thicket. They must

move organs aside to cut away whatever can't

be saved from my gentle father. What I heard

didn't sound like my friend, with whom, only hours

before, I sat, laughing. Night stretches out over the rows

of rooftops like a sheet spread out over

the country. It sounded like an animal. *I'm here*, I say

to myself, running my fingers down the length

of my torso as if pulling on a zipper.

heart of the poem

Strata

You don't understand, he says again,
from the back seat of the car, my son

who only months ago could not fall
asleep before whispering, first, some

secret in my ear. When I look
in the rearview, he turns toward peaks

in the distance, and when I ask him
to explain, shaking his head, he sighs as if

it isn't worth the trouble. I had
the same words for my father, and one day,

cursing, pushed him through the doorway
with the full strength of the body I had

grown into. At forty-five, he could
have pinned me to the wall, but at

what cost? It's a story we don't like
to tell. My son and I ride in silence

until he asks how long it takes
to get there, an apology in the sound

of his voice if not the words. I do
understand. *Not long*, I say, as we drive

through desert mountains that have stood
for six million years, and which I once thought

looked like the fallen bodies of giants,
gods grown over with yellow grass.

poignant imagery, fav line

In the book we are reading together,

the father dies before the first
sentence: *Nnamdi didn't want to look*

at his body in the casket. We pass it back
and forth, taking turns, our heads

casting shadows onto the page. Early on
the father returns from the dead as

a shadow in the street. *Is it really him?*
When they speak, we speak the way

we imagine they'd sound, angry or sad.
Sometimes I get to be the son, and you're

the dad. Sometimes you sound
the letters out until a word reveals

itself—new. You stare off as if you know
how the book will come together. You look

at my face as if you can see the sounds
it makes. Sometimes you grow bored

and want to stop. Sometimes you wonder if
the father is gone for good. You yawn.

It's getting late. We are coming to
the last page, and I nod along. Soon

we'll see where the story has
taken us. Sometimes you want

a story to last forever, and sometimes
you just want to know how it ends.

The Conversion

You picked them this morning from
a tree in the corner of the yard. You liked the way

the stem gave to your pull, how the branch lifted,
the scent of rinds, after, on your hands.

In Caravaggio's *Conversion on the Way*
to Damascus, the man, fallen from

his horse onto the road, eyes closed, lifts his hands
into the light, pushing away, grasping—which

is it?—the source of his illumination, which
you cannot see. You place the bowl of lemons

in the middle of the table. Look
how bright they shine. Don't look.

Ten Years Before I Met You

I'd never get there, past
the butcher shop, the church,
the station, where trains came and went,
almost empty, the bar full
by midmorning. A path up the hill
from which you could see
the whole city—I would go
one day. In winter, the sky
became a wall, the snow never-ending.
Waiting for the bus, no one spoke
English. When it came, late and full,
it stopped, but the doors
did not open. Some nights, I stood
in the orange booth, calling out
to anyone who would answer. I grew lean
over the months, shedding what
I brought but didn't need
until my loneliness became
beautiful, whetting a want
inside me, and when the row
of cottonwoods that lined the streets
bloomed in March, their seeds
floated through the air, a nuisance, but
like a dream. A gift from—

whom? Someone tried
to tell me once. I cannot
remember. I didn't understand.

Anniversary

At the end of the street, we came upon La Capilla
del Santo Cristo de la Salud, a chapel begun

in 1753. The year before, Baltazar
Montanez lost control of his mount and plunged

over the cliffs. In that moment, Secretary Don
Mateo Prats called from a balcony, *Christ*

of good health, save him. The horse didn't survive,
but the young rider did. People come to pray

for cures, the chapel adorned with oils
by Jose Campeche and silver ornaments

depicting parts of the body: legs, heart, arms, lungs.
Open on Tuesdays only, we couldn't go inside,

but noted pictures on placards. We sipped juice
from straws, and he leaned out to look over the ledge

where waves crashed against the stone wall. *A long
way down,* he said with a shudder, and I agreed.

The Good Guy

We stood on the back porch in the late
afternoon, crying hard but quiet so

the kids wouldn't hear, and looked at
each other. After, tired, we fell asleep

on the couch, which we hadn't done
in years. When we moved into this house,

we found a garden, and that first summer,
I picked tomatoes, squash, my hands

passing over what needed more time,
what had fallen to the ground, rotting or

half-eaten. When the season ended, we
let the grass spread over the dirt and

whatever else was buried there. I woke up
in the early evening to a sadness

like something I could point to, a painting
you hung on the wall, a silver bowl

you filled with coins from countries you might
never see again. I could hear the boys

playing in the next room—*Now, I get
to be the bad guy*, until one stopped

the game to say, *I'm hungry.*
Me, too, the other said, and you got up

slowly and made your way to the kitchen.

The Hummingbird

A blur in the periphery,
like the mind if the mind

were airborne, a buzz among
leaf and orange blossom,

the long beak pressing quick
into flower after flower, high

on each sweet center, and
each iridescent feather shines

hard—a thought, half-formed,
charged, a hum before it lights

on the branch—and you
see it clearly—dimmed, now,

small, no longer what it was.

Notes

"On What Has Become of His Body"

The lines from this poem were taken from David Keplinger's *The Long Answer: New and Selected Poems.*

Title: page 141

Section 1: pages 38, 120, 42, 43, 115, 167, 45, 31, 34, 108, 27, 113, 28, 21

Section 2: pages 21, 22, 152, 157, 152, 133, 131, 134, 131, 32, 35, 124, 18, 168

Section 3: pages 168, 134, 46, 132, 131, 44, 114, 105, 38, 106, 44, 111, 115, 135

Acknowledgements:

Gratitude to the editors of the following publications, where many of these poems first appeared: Academy of American Poets Poem-a-Day, *Adroit, The American Poetry Review, Cherry Tree, Crazyhorse, Five South, The Georgia Review, Green Mountains Review, Kenyon Review, New England Review, Notre Dame Review, Orion, Pleiades, Prairie Schooner, TAB: The Journal of Poetry & Poetics,* and *Terrain.*

"Fatherland" was also featured in *Dear America: Letters of Hope, Habitat, Defiance, and Democracy* and Ours Poetica (Poetry Foundation).

For their guidance, I want to thank Sandra Alcosser, Kazim Ali, Dulce Arteaga, Karen Harryman, David Keplinger, Vandana Khanna, Grace Li, Helena Mesa, Shannon K. Winston, and most of all, Joseph Cassell. Also, for their support, my sincere gratitude to Francisco Aragón, Sandra Beasley, Cyrus Cassells, Stephanie Dugger, Kate Gale, Oliver de la Paz, and everyone at the Community of Writers, Napa Valley Writers Conference, and Four Way Books, of course, especially Ryan Murphy and Martha Rhodes, who have done so much to bring this book and so many others out into the world.

Blas Falconer is the author of *Forgive the Body This Failure, The Foundling Wheel,* and *A Question of Gravity and Light* as well as the coeditor of two anthologies, *Mentor and Muse: Essays from Poets to Poets* and *The Other Latin@: Writing Against a Singular Identity*. The recipient of a poetry fellowship from the National Endowment for the Arts and a Maureen Egen Writers Exchange Award from *Poets & Writers*, he teaches in San Diego State University's MFA program and is the editor in chief at *Poetry International Online*.

WE ARE ALSO GRATEFUL TO THOSE INDIVIDUALS WHO PARTICIPATED IN OUR
BUILD A BOOK PROGRAM. THEY ARE:

Anonymous (14), Robert Abrams, Debra Allbery, Nancy Allen,
Michael Ansara, Kathy Aponick, Jean Ball, Sally Ball, Jill Bialosky,
Sophie Cabot Black, Laurel Blossom, Tommye Blount, Karen and
David Blumenthal, Jonathan Blunk, Lee Briccetti, Jane Martha Brox,
Mary Lou Buschi, Anthony Cappo, Carla and Steven Carlson,
Robin Rosen Chang, Liza Charlesworth, Peter Coyote, Elinor Cramer,
Kwame Dawes, Michael Anna de Armas, Brian Komei Dempster,
Renko and Stuart Dempster, Matthew DeNichilo, Rosalynde Vas Dias,
Patrick Donnelly, Charles R. Douthat, Lynn Emanuel, Blas Falconer,
Laura Fjeld, Carolyn Forché, Helen Fremont and Donna Thagard,
Debra Gitterman, Dorothy Tapper Goldman, Alison Granucci,
Elizabeth T. Gray Jr., Naomi Guttman and Jonathan Meade,
Jeffrey Harrison, KT Herr, Carlie Hoffman, Melissa Hotchkiss,
Thomas and Autumn Howard, Catherine Hoyser, Elizabeth Jackson,
Linda Susan Jackson, Jessica Jacobs, Deborah Jonas-Walsh, Jennifer Just,
Voki Kalfayan, Maeve Kinkead, Victoria Korth, David Lee and
Jamila Trindle, Rodney Terich Leonard, Howard Levy, Owen Lewis and
Susan Ennis, Eve Linn, Matthew Lippman, Ralph and Mary Ann Lowen,
Maja Lukic, Neal Lulofs, Anthony Lyons, Ricardo Alberto Maldonado,
Trish Marshall, Donna Masini, Deborah McAlister, Carol Moldaw,
Michael and Nancy Murphy, Kimberly Nunes, Matthew Olzmann and
Vivee Francis, Veronica Patterson, Patrick Phillips, Robert Pinsky,
Megan Pinto, Kevin Prufer, Anna Duke Reach, Paula Rhodes,
Yoana Setzer, James Shalek, Soraya Shalforoosh, Peggy Shinner,
Joan Silber, Jane Simon, Debra Spark, Donna Spruijt-Metz, Arlene Stang,
Page Hill Starzinger, Catherine Stearns, Yerra Sugarman, Arthur Sze,
Laurence Tancredi, Marjorie and Lew Tesser, Peter Turchi, Connie Voisine,
Susan Walton, Martha Webster and Robert Fuentes, Calvin Wei,
Allison Benis White, Lauren Yaffe, and Rolf Yngve.

Made in the USA
Las Vegas, NV
07 September 2024

94853496R00049